Dotard

(Poems)

UZOMA C. NDUKA

DOTARD

Dotard

(Poems)

Published by

Brain-Box Books

64 Mbonu Street, D-Line, Port
Harcourt, Rivers State, Nigeria.
Tel: 08056451880
E-mail: brainboxbooks@gmail.com

Copyright © Uzoma C. Nduka

ISBN: 978-198-058-2816

Dedication

For Ngozi Sylvia Nduka

Acknowledgement

This work would not have been possible without the guidance of the Holy Spirit. Thank you, Lord!

I am especially indebted to my friends over the years and who are members of the Zenith Family Network. Thanks to Boris Orji (MD), Bidwell Okere, Gerald Ibe (Biafra), Nnamdi Osuagwu, Eke Uguru, Onyii Wamah, Chuma Onwudiwe, Ifeatu Onwuasoanya, Prof. Bond Anyaehie, Poks Ucheaguwa, Christopher Okafor, George Ukaegbu, Wellington Ogude, Tony Ononye, Emenike, Ikenna Otti, Ifeanyi, and others too numerous to mention.

I am grateful to all I have had the pleasure to associate with since my sojourn in the US: Victor Ikechy Gab-Ojukwu and Ozioma (Doctor mu) Thelma Gab-Ojukwu (MD), Emeka Boris Orji (MD), Sir Chris Ukelonu, Uche Odoemenam, Aida Tekla, Dr. Eji Nwuke, Augustine Obinna (MD) & wife, Bishop Ade Ajala, Paschal Eze, Ven. & Mrs Ugo Okoroafor (Dee), Emeka Okocha, Fred Nnanna and Uju, Ifeanyi Nwobodo (MD), Oluwaseun Ogungbele, Leo Agwu, Chibuzor Iheaka, and Olu Oduneye.

Let me add Happy Agbeyi, Omeregie Godwin, John Ibazhoba, Ete, John Aikpokpo, Uchechukwu Christian, Charles Duku and Osaze Osemwegie-Ero.

A special thanks to Prof. Martins U. Nwankwo, Profs. Isidore Diala, JohnClife Nwadike, Omen-Maduka Durunze, M.C. Onukawa and Dr. Ogbonna Onuoha. As my teachers and mentors, they have taught me more than I could ever give them credit for here. Dr. Uche Emelonye, Obi Emelonye and Azubuike Erinugha.

I am grateful to the management and staff of Denver Human Services: Don Mares, Jay Morein, Todd Jorgensen, and Larraine Archuleta. Mayor Michael Hancock, the innovative mayor of the City and County is not left out. Thank you Susan Radaelli and Andi Blaustein.

Thanks to Moses Nduka, Lemmy Nduka, Chinedu Nduka, Chief Randy Nduka, Chaze Nze, Ugo Onuoha, Obina Nwokorie, Patience Akhihiero and Dorothy Ileleji.

My eternal gratitude to my parents whose love and guidance are with me in whatever I pursue. They are the ultimate role models. Most important thanks to

Ngoo, and my extremely wonderful daughter, Somma ("Maama") Onyeoma ("Zitelu") for their unending inspiration.

Table of Contents

SECTION 1: LOVE

SECTION 2: POLITICS

SECTION 3: SPRIRITUAL

SECTION 4: SOCIAL

Love

UNQUANTIFIABLE

You gave me
Immeasurable gift of life
Which comes from a
Clean heart, and
Unmodulated soul, the
Gift so inestimable, gift
So, unquestionable, so
Unquantifiable
You said you will, and Yes,
you did what you said It
came to be a never felt
Before touch, my Soul
was touched
My heart was touched
You, only you have
Have ever done this to me,
Unquantifiable. Unquestionable.
Immeasurable. This gift: Prayers

SWEETNESS

My dear sweetness
The glow in you
Twists my thoughts
In show of love
To you I swear
To hold and touch
All lifelong

My dear sweetness
You came to me
When eclipse came
And shown your lights
With all in you
And now I am
All yours I am

Dear sweetness
In you I have
A perfect match
My rib in you
Completes my being
I'll say the same
All day long

DOTARD

Dear sweetness
Each day I live
With you in me
I deeply say
How lucky I am
To have a gem
As great as you

My sweet sweetness
Take all of me
And make them yours
My heart my soul
Your hands to save
In time before and life to come
Yours I am
Here I am

BABY, TAKE MY LIFE

Take my life
Let it be
Solemnly. Solely,
My life to you
Take my minutes
Take my seconds,
Let them flow
In ceaseless form
Let them flow
In endless way

Take my hands
Let them transmit
At the whim
Of your love
Take my feet
Let them be
Swift,
Stunning for you
Swift,
Lovely for you

DOTARD

Take my voice
Let me sing
Continuously. Constantly
Only for you
Take my lips
Let them be
Packed with passages
Only for you
Filled with frottage
Just for you

Take my naira
Take my euro
Not a kobo
Would I keep
Take my brain
Use it all
Every power
As you may
Every hour
As you want

Take my will
Make it yours
It will be

No more mine
Take my heart
It is yours. Yours alone
Let it be
Your royal throne
It will be
Your noble cathedra

Take my love
My love I pour,
At your feet
Its treasure-store,
Take my being
I will be
Ever always
All for you
Ever always
All for you

WHAT IF

What if I give you my heart to keep
Will you keep it in a safe place?
Or will you keep it where hawks prey
What if I give you my heart to keep?

It seems to me that you will keep my heart in
yours But I still wonder how safe your own heart is
It seems to me so brittle and fragile It
makes me wonder, what if it breaks

If my heart breaks in your hands
Will you be able to mend it?
How good will it look when you mend it?
Just to know: what if?

I wish you didn't have a brittle heart
So, every time you have my heart
I will go to sleep, sleep so deep
And forget what if the world ends

Tell me you have a heart of gold
So, I can rest my restless heart

And know that in your heart My
own heart is safe and sound

What if my heart is safe and sound?
Your brittle heart will be in mine
And safely will I keep your heart
And make it mine forever more

DRUNKEN EYES

I looked into your drunken eyes
I saw some smoke push through your eyes
The thoughts of which were fresh to me
And made me think you were mine

I scanned through your twinkly brain
I saw some sparks inside of it
They walked into my ready heart
As if she knew where she belonged

Though held too close into your arms
I felt I knew where I called home
Inside these smoky fiery eyes
Inside this sparkling thoughtful brain

Thoughts of it made me fear
The red blood cells through your eyes
But calm I was when it came
So silently into my heart

DOTARD

Now I know where to call home
No more fear inside my house
No more tears in his arms
All but calm, I will feel

GO HUG THE TREE

For you, I've caught hot fire
For you, I've jumped off the cliff
For you, I've fought the priest
For you, I've stayed long hours

In Colorado's 25 inches blizzard
And 130 degrees Arizona sun
Outside the rippling, Oklahoma tornado
During the California draining drought

All for you!
But you've tossed me out from our apartment
You have always tossed 911 all over me
You have branded me drunk and promiscuous
You have named me all manners of name

I ditched my friends, just for you
I'm so faithful to our cause
Yet you snob and trash me
Yet you cast me away like an outcast

You've accused me of not loving
you And told me I drugged you

DOTARD

You've accused me of cheating
Yet, I'm with you day in and out

I've proven to you that I'm straight
I've shown you I'm by your side
I've done to you what no man could
do I've chosen you over others

Yet, you ditched me.
Go hug a tree!

I LOVE THIS GIRL

I loved this girl, right from the start
The very first day, I set my eyes on her
I felt a huge spark right inside my head
I turned, I spun, and I wheeled my head to every route
I swear to you, I acted like an imbecile
I thought I was a dude, not until I saw her radiance
I stood, I sat, I peeped, and I craned just to get her attention
But she was focused on something else
I hissed, I whistled, I made some noise with empty bottles
Yet, she sat unmoved, untouched, unperturbed about the noises
I sat in awe of her beauty

Wanting to be seen
I walked up to the disc jockey
Told him to play my favorite
But my favorite song did not catch her attention
I danced alone on the dancing floor
Thinking I will be recognized
Yet, that did not attract this beauty's sympathy

I gazed in the air, started starring straight at her
I winked, I blew an empty kiss to her: empty kiss it
was
I wrinkled a paper, where I wrote my number, threw
it at her table
I thought I was in trouble but she ignored me
Days passed, weeks trickled by, then I saw
I saw this request, request to be
accepted As a Facebook friend

Quickly, I did
Quickly, I called
Quickly, we bonded
Quickly, she's mine
I love this girl

TEN SHADES OF CRAZE

Love in the
Air is love lost

When love is
Blind it's not love

Faith without
Work is faith dead

Faith unseen
Is hope to come

Silence in
Crisis is just crime

Silence is
Golden but isn't dumb

Shout in
Ashkelon is not noise

Garb of
Unity is us all

IMPRISONED

The walls of your
Heart have gagged this
Rock mind of mine

In the dark places
Of my heart, your
Tender tendons have torn down those
dark ligaments

These dark ligaments leading
shadiness ashore to the place
Of light, and graciousness into blankness

You have still toed
Into this narrow crevice
And cemented the gaps with affordable
arable affection

The lust in me
Transubstantiated into lush love
Like the divine sacrifice of one's own son

DOTARD

Your triumphant entrance into
My being makes me
Wear a new face of righteousness

Take me, take me
To the hollows of
Your lockup, let me be your lasting lone lifer

DANGEROUSLY DEADLY

I heard this is a game
A game played with unseen arms
But are able to
Pierce through tiny veins and arteries

I was told it's dicey
So dangerous that players
Are so oblivious of its
Returns and retorts

I was naive to expert advice
And was expecting I could turn the tables
And make a mark no one has made
And be the superhero of our time

Now, I guess I'm a fool
For holding on to extant stance
And in this instance, I was
Absolutely naive and native

DOTARD

I was in it to die for it
I never knew she was in it to gain from it
I was absolutely naive and native
I didn't know it was dangerous

I was told my heart could explode I
was told my castle could crash I
was shown the danger I was in But,
I guess, I was naive and native

In my dreams, I saw you hide your face
I saw crushing scars all over my face
I brush them off as a mere dream
Not knowing that the experts are right

Inside of me, I thought I would make it
right I fought so hard to see it fly
But she was there to suck it dry
So naive I was, so native I am

CRUCIFIED

I came to you
Naked and pure
But you let the
World taint your brain
And you hated me

I came to you
With a heart, contrite and
broken You allowed your mind
To conjure and construe blackmail against me

I came to you
At a time, divine design was at work
But you listened to the walls
And they fed you with falsehoods and
You were bought over

I came to you
With untainted love
Love that counts no errors
But you rejected me and threw me
Into the dustbin of condemnation
Here I am

Destroyed
Here I am
Damaged
Here I am
Lost
Here I am
Alone
Here I am

At the intersection of life
Crucified and punctured
I'm deflated
I'm defeated
I'm done

Good night
Until the heavens open
And if we are to
Meet again by divine design
We will then meet
Good night
Till we meet again

OUVRIR

This woman is way too fecund
With womb so fertile
Worthwhile for worthy suitors
Vegetative for willing visitors
From the village or from the city
From within or without
With lice on your head
Or poop in your underpants
She's open, very, very open
Inside her ovaries are grown
Waiting for semen to own
From end to end she shows
The beauty therein
From time to time she says
I'm the one to behold
Her bust is filled with gold
Her stump, so green and pure
Her hips remain the attraction
Her butt, so hard to forget
In her, are so much meat
With her, your coast is clear
In search of where to breathe
There's room in her long lung

No junk. No chuck. No muck.
From east of her waist
To south of her neck
No junk. No chuck. No muck.
Her Westside is high premium
Her north pole, up in price
No matter your way in
The roads to heart are open
This woman is too fecund
This woman is still virgin
Come serve yourself some lunch

I'VE GOT YOU BABE

You did read my incapacities
And provided me wheelchair
To ride in, till I get to my
Destination, with you as my helper.

You did know how frail I was
When you saw the scales fall
Off my skin, yet you carefully
Threaded them back like a seamstress.

You saw all my defalcations
And loaned to my locked ears words
That sailed gently down my
Cerebrum like an intravenous nitrate.

You heard all my mechanical defects
Yet, you assembled my partitioned
parts, Waxed out corrosive dints from
Deep inside my combustible mix.

Now you are down, like old age,
I wish to whisper into your vaults
The words you spoke, and more,
I've got you till the end of time.

Political

CHANCES ARE

Chances are we were hoodwinked on that gloomy rainy day
When we all stood in line for hours with our broken umbrellas
Abandoned our sick children in dilapidated sunken sick berths
And put our thumbs on tattered papers for elusive change

Chances are we all boarded some swindlers car
Driven by masked men whose profession is to manacle masses
And trade, sow, and usurp open opportunities of fear
To create escalating and increasing fear in all of us

Chances are that there was no real *Boko Haram* as sold
Chances are that there was no real bring-back-our-girls match as seen
Chances are that all were tinkered, tutored to further steal from us
The act that they have truly perfected through all apparatuses of power

Chances are we will continue to fall for them each
time the bell jingles
We fall in line over again not knowing what we are
falling in line for
We put our thumbs down to their deceitful,
deranged symbols again
Just bamboozled, baffled by bags of rice and poor
pieces of naira

Chances are we won't wash our eyes clean the next
time
We will sidetrack our consciences and consciousness
And stroll to the pauperized pulverized polling
stations
And vote the same old shameless men

Chances are we will never learn from our piloted past
A past that had drained our imaginations, images
and being
Confused, contoured, constrained our way of life
And stationed, stopped, stuck us all in an immobile
derailing demo-c-rats" disease

RATE YOUR LEADERS

Failures. Thieves. Robbers.
Unpatriotic. Cultists. Cabals. Non-
conformists. Deaf. Dullards.
Nonsuccess. Looters. Fraudsters.
Guzzlers. Callous. Indifferent.
Wicked. Uncaring. Devilish.
Dishonorable. Dishonest. Dupes.
Unprincipled. Uncivilized.
Flagitious. Shameless. Delinquent.
Bankrupt. Sadistic. Wolfish.
Uncultured. Nefarious. Diabolical.
Deadly. Atrocious. Damned.
Barbaric. Deplorable. Pestilential.
Black. Dark. Poisonous. Creepy

CAPITOL HELL

Once in a while, they call it a hill
For its crooked cusps and curves
Deep inside, are dirt of sorts
Rotten, rancid, putrid, and all
The feet of which kill all the bills
The top above, crush all the dreams
When we think we have some hopes
They quash and trash our sweats and treats.
Just to save them some more terms,
They sell their souls on Wall Street road
Just like thieves, they stash our wealth
And wire them all to offshore vaults
This place is hell and smell like hell
With constant strollers, in and out
The door revolves to their own gain
And never choke them with all these loots
Some day will come, we shall prevail
What we say is all in vain
Until that day when hell will hail

DON'T FAIL ME

I know myself
So full of ideas
Not fears not tears
But true to the core
I have been called
Bride of all nations
I have been dubbed

Land of our gods
But since a few seconds
The stories I hear
Isn't of good taste
They make me puke
Riffraff from midriff
I walk the streets
And get their boos
I fly the air
My tail, they aim
I sail the sea
Their prick, they set
I hang on the moon
They push my limit
I'm no more cherished

DOTARD

By my old schoolmates
I'm no more loved
By high school loves
Each time I'm awake
I hear some shit stuff
And they go viral
To all the end places
Each time I turn on
My old black *teevee*.
All I do hear
Is doom and gloom
All I have touched
Beggars and paupers
All I have felt

Are pain and disdain
All I have touched
Distress and warfare
The sounds are too sad
To be my trademark
All I have built
All through these years
Seems to crash soon
In one sole sweep
My sweat and my toil

DOTARD

All turn to sports
All they have done
Sow fears and tears
All they have done
Tear down my pride
All they have done
Pour blood and soil
In one fell swoop
My wisdom they crush
All through these years
Seems to crash down

STORY TIME

Once upon a time
There was a man named Dumb
He claimed to be so smart
As smart as cat and rat
He saw himself as all
Knew everything on earth
Dumb drummed himself atop
With lies and stuff made up
He told his own a lot
A lot of things untrue
He forged himself so nice
Packaging of some sort
A lot fell for his tales
Tales not told by moonlight
Because those tales aren't good
Nothing to learn from them
The tales berate some folks
And put others on edge
No one had balls enough
To tell him in his face
How stale those tales appear
With no human appeal
The fly is now on the scrotum

No one knows what to do
To kill or not to kill, but
I know in time so near
We all will see the head
The head of this deal so bad
Served us in broad daylight
With eyes so wide and clear
And ears not clogged with much
We fell for this dumb *Dumb*
Who tipped his heaps of trash
On our face and space
In front of our own yards
And left our barns bereaved
We wail and cry each day
Hoping the best should come
From those in charge of law
But all we see is worse
Worse than what Dumb has drummed
We see our men like wimps
All whine and whine and whine
Our hopes as thin as razor
Fade quickly in our eyes
By drums that cannot talk
And gongs bitten by ants
Both losing their weak voices

And drowned by river Dumb
In time to come we'll know
How deep we've dug this
hole In time to come we'll
know How back we moved
the post In time to come we'll
know How bad this time had
been This tale is told by me A
witness of this history

HE KNEW WHAT HE SIGNED UP FOR
(In honor of all US soldiers killed in action-KIA)

I never knew
I will hear this
Even in my casket
Laying so cold
Wrapped with colors
Hugged by beloved
Seen and unseen
I went into this
To honor all sacrifices
Made by my forefathers
Who fought so gallantly
To grant me freedom
To give me the chance
To defend and honor
This great nation
Yet, I was scorned
Scorned in death
Disdained in life
Yet, I was burned
My wife, my kids, my unborn
We have been buried
Dead and alive

We have been dealt
The final nail
I never knew
We will descend
This low
Not in this century
Not in my country
Not from someone
I fight to guard
With my life
With my blood
Everyday
Of my life
I knew what I
Signed up for
But you shouldn't
Tell me that
Even when I'm no more

RODENTS

I woke up this morning to discover how powerful
rodents are
In my native land where we have all manners of jolly
jujumen
And million miracle workers and potent prayer
warriors
Who should have dissolved the powerless power of
rodents with Holy Ghost fire

Chances are that witches and wizards in Abuja House
in London lost
Their potency by soiling their hands with parking
fees and hospital fees
And propaganda fees to offshore accounts instead
of inshore accounts via rodent routing number
And with that vexation, rodents declared all-out war
for reneging on business agreement

Chances are we believe that these rodents were sent
by the witches and wizards
In my native land, so that we will not have any trace
of how much has been wasted in

Oversea hospital trip by our elected officials and
their entourages and that way
The accountant-general can cook-up new gazillion
ill-gazette expenditure and present to us

Another thing is this, those rats were sent to damage
everything that has been brought to
Light before the return of the man whose home has
been ravaged by rodents so that our crime
Commission will have nothing to fall back on when
the reckoning time comes and
We will resort to saying that it was all fake news after
all and it was the work of enemies

I am also thinking that the rats were sent by
sycophants who want to portray to the world
That we are really idiots and that we don't know that
there's no way rats can penetrate
Through underground tunnels leading into the
walled-in office without passing through
Several guards and fortes and electric fences and
bullet-proof gates

I also think that these sycophants sent these rats to
damage this place

These sycophants are trying to avoid a repeat of
history so that they can solidly
Get their acts together in case the worst happens
which someday will happen when it will happen

VUM, VAM

Billions *vum*
Millions *vam*

Vam to Bermuda
Vum to Cyprus

They *vum*
And *vam*

To places unknown
To hideouts below

They *vum*
They *vam*

To climates so cold
And stay their till old

They *vum*
They vam

With our milk and plum
And use it for porn

Since way back
We know

They *vum*
They *vam*

They borrow from
Foreign vault

And *vum*
And *vam*

They burrow our
Well-beings

And *vum*
And *vam*

Before our
Own eyes

They *vum*
They *vam*

DOTARD

In their farms
They *vum*

In thick forests
They *vam*

They *vam* us
In billions

And very soon
In trillions

And that time
We will know

That we've been *vummed*
And we've been *vammed*

They *vum*
They *vam*

CRY, MY COUNTRYMEN

Cry, my countrymen
Cry, my beloved
Cry, my fellow citizens
Cry, my people

We cry from deep inside
We cry from our hearts
We cry our eyes out
We cry and cry and cry

We cry for the rots
We cry for decades of decay
We cry against stressed strengths
We cry for these nut jobs

Our tears are from within
Our fears are from outside
We cry in unison
For our unity is threatened

From far, from wide
From near, from dear
We cry and cry
We cry, so real

DOTARD

In real time
Our tears flow
And is measured
With jagged tools

To all ears
We cry
But no one
Replies

It's too sad
To say
That our fate
Is gone

We cry for ourselves
We cry for our kids
We cry for our kin
We cry for our people

Our people in dungeons
Littered in all corners
Of our own love:
Cry, my countrymen, cry

ANATOMY OF POETRY

The nice
The vice
The voice

From soft
To hard
The heart

The smooth
And rough
In mind

Of crime
The crème
The called

In files
They fall
And fail

The saved
The savior

Our saints
Of sorrow
And sadness
And pity

Their joy
Their sports
Their gain

We cry
We lay
And waste

Our voice
We lend
For free

Our gain
We trade
For loss

We seat
We watch
We submit

They plunge

DOTARD

With glee
Our thumbs
They ruin
Our sense
And self

Our voice
They nip
And trip

We play
We pray
We cry

We pay
With blood
And tears

The next
Of us
Not known

Our bread
Our tills
May die

DOTARD

The crumbs
The cross
May eclipse

Our hopes
Our faith
Are wrong

Of guile
Of graft
And glee

We sit
We pray
They play

Of all
Of these
For them

In time
In tomb
We will

DOTARD

These lines
Though few
And far

These lines
So loaded
With thoughts

One day
You drink
From here

One day
You read
These rhymes

Of nice
Of vice
And voice

Your voice
Your might
Your power

DOTARD

Some day
All these
Will end

All these
Some day
So soon

The sum
Of these
Some day

All these
Some day
Will sum

SCREED

Flipping through this man's moribund mind

Meaningless thoughts running in and out his enclosed encephalon

Screaming side to side, in every sideway, no segue no symmetry

Casting itself on distant eye lookers and inside butt lickers

The pages and folios of his mind burns from time to time

Each constantly characterized by uncertainties and gullibility

His head hideously modified by unseen hands

And things, he or she or "it" he comes in last contact with

Scared to the pants, screams embarrassingly on onlookers

The search getting into his crotch, the touch of which, from

Those he deems unfit to, seems not too comfy

His multi-colored nature begins to peel off layer by layer

Each strata of his skin smells of rot from the butt

But he seems to defend each band of lies with self-implicating

Tweet, the peel of each unveils his most hidden hits

That has been kept mum and away from public glare

Inside their hearts, they glee at his rumbling empty brain

They clap and cheer and urge him on to let himself

Drive into his own ditch by himself and against himself:

Just helping him achieve his own crooked dream from crooked deals

With a deaf right ear, he hears not the smell of his mucks

And now, he sacks the keeper of secrets and let his hands

Run before his brain, and his brain not too quick to discern, ignites

His pointed mouth to run amuck and now this is where he is

A place where the notorious squat, a place where deplorable perch, a

Place where non-populists burn, he knows not his fate, so

He shoots his catapult in all directions, hoping his unrefined arrow

Sticks into someone's anus and they will all fall together

But, gradually, the house is disintegrating, noticing

The eventual demise of the architect of his own failure, sensing

The inevitable that will befall him from the hands of the special

Prosecutor who knows not his fate but is speedy at work

Now, digging into the screeds of this rumbling raucous rambunctious

Mind, the long monotonous harangue of a man hoping to

Hide his horrendous lifestyle and marriage with Kremlin

But tells us there's no such intercourse, time will tell!

FOR 240 YEARS...

For 240 years
And enumerating
We have
Only loused
Up nations
And bollixed up
Their consciousness
Upside down
Charged constantly
Like roaring
Lion at
Sleeping sheep
Strewing their
Streets with
Corrupt carcasses
For 240 years

For 240 years
Till today,
We have,
In crates
And bullions,
Consigned billions

And trillions
Over to
Other nations
AWOL. Unexplained
Humanitarian assistance
Humpty dumpty
Gone. Unrestored
We give
They give
Contraceptives. Condoms
Build exotic
Princely palaces
Marry virgins
In twelves
Crown themselves
Kings. Queens
Till today

For 240 years
And surging
We have
Left our
Own in
Homelessness and
Roofless tops

In search
When they
Return from
Democracy defense
Apostles of
State creed
Our own
Are here
In search
For cure
Yet we
Keep exporting
To miles
Unknown. We
Keep moving
This cure
While ours
Beg for
Stipends trimonthly
Every six
Months, every
Year, begging
All seasons
For 240 years
For 240 years

We have
Treated ours
Like outcasts
Throwing them
Away like
Swine, asking
Them.
Them to do
What they
Cannot do
For the
Nation, sacrifice:

For 240 years
You assemble
In the
House of
The privileged
And spew
All lies
All untruths
All falsehood
About your
Patriotism to
Moneybags over

Nation's interest
They line
Your pockets
In Bermuda
And Cyprus
And you
Mount the
Rostrum to
Tell me
To give
And it
Shall be
Given unto
Me: what
Have you
Given: to
This nation

For 240 years
You have
Sowed seeds
Of discord
Of discomfort
Of disharmony
Of hate

Of anger
Of evil
Across red
States and
Blue states
Over the
Pacific and
The deep
Blue seas
You have
Moved armored
Cars to
Destroy cultures
And castles
To demolish
Ancient gods
And establish
Your gods

For 240 years
You have
Told; sold
Them this
Thing you
Call democracy

Commodity cleared
By your
Customs and
Not accepted
As their
Custom; like
Cancer, it
Rejects every
Injection, yet
You persist
You insist
You sell
You tell:
That this
Thing is
The medicine
For all

For 240 years
It's all
Emptiness and
Promises; promises
Not kept
You lie
We line

DOTARD

You sell
We buy
Empty promises
For 240 years

SHE CRIES
(The Agony of a Child Who Lost Her Father).

The cry of a little girl, she
Cries. She cries for a nation
That has learned to dishonor her own. She cries.
Even when they bring glory to her
And defend her. She cries.
Against enemies within and without. She cries. She
cries for a land that abandons her warriors And
fighters, who in alien world engage in battle of
freedoms, battle
Of brain over brawl. She cries.
She cries for tears are there.
She cries.
More and more and more
She cries.
For freedom eludes her in the land
That she was born into, the land
That has told her she is second.
She cries.
For the red hills of Georgia are no longer there.
Hills and valleys are still high and not low.
State of Mississippi is still sweltering with heat
of injustice.

Rough places have never been made plain.
The glory of God not yet revealed. All dreams.
She cries.
She cries for a country
That has called her names and has not said I'm sorry.
She cries.
For sins of her unknowing
Past, sins so unforgettable.
She cries.
She cries for a country that has come to hush
others due
To the color of their skins.
She cries. And the tears were no more
She cries. And accepts her faith.
She knew what she signed for.
She cries. And her father was no more.
No one listens to the content of her father's
character.
She weeps.

ADOPTION VS SANCTION

Little lines of rhyme
Told by luxury liars
In bid to hide the scoop
They dig themselves a ditch
No matter how they try
To wave this one away
No matter what they say
No whiff, a whiff, some whiffs
The lies under their belts
Will tell us who they are
The guiles inside their lips
Will guide us to that closet
The closet with the truth
About these empty rhymes
That make no sense at all
But make some sense to some
Their several changing gears
Will drive them to their graves
No, not to graves
But find themselves in pinfold
There, they will stay and say
These little lines of lies

DOTARD

Have brought us to our knees
These whooping wildest whoopers
Have made us fall from grace
Little lines of rhymes
A whiff, some whiff, huge whiff

WHITE MEN LIE TOO

Men of value, they claim
Yet they grope and dope
Every day, they sing
America, the land of free
In every way they gag
Children with no
Faults of theirs
Every day they say
Go back you aliens
Tell me who you fool
You dopes, you gropes, you rogues
You rob from down the books
And claim it is right to do
You kill each bill in place
To keep you out of space
Each cent for us you cross
And pass it on to the rich
Each dime for time you kill
And take it home for pork's
Yet you sing and say
America, land of free
Tell me why you lie
As the circle turns to four

DOTARD

To everyone you lie
To win their votes in droves
In every year, you lie
Your name gets stamped to it
The future will one day say
Here lies the liars-in-mischief

IAMBIC PENTAMETER

Shall I compare this shameless generation to many old honorable men who stood for this entrapment but this entrapment never stood for them?

Shall I say these strange bedfellows are more deceitful and more inchoate than devil and his evil cohorts?

Little winds do show their empty anuses that produce loud noises that mean harm to their clan's men and women.

Sometimes, too hot the knives of old, sharply sharpened by the old blacksmith strike into their blind eyes and make them as blind a bat as they originally were and like sheep they bleat and wander around rudderless.

By choice, not chance, they stole the credit of old and lavished it on mansions and ill missions of their handiwork hoping that their handicapped thinking will escape the wrath of the future.

One day, nature will change course on you and unleash its untrimmed spokes along with its poisonous venom upon your ovulated heart and burgeoning body and deflate it six feet under.

Then your winding witchcraft will fade and lose possession of our polity and dwell in the land of the unmentioned for you have injured us too many.

As far as we have women with fertile wombs that will give birth to strong men who have breathed the air of this ideology or have seen the dreams of their forefathers, so long as these lives live and breathe, so shall this dream live and breathe and give life to lives that shall live and breathe.

I HOPE

I hope we dance, not
The python's dance
Which eats up the living.
Modern anomaly. Our reality.

I hope we dance
Like the honeybees
Which can waggle dance
And pass silent sentences as they buzz

I hope we smile, not
Like the crocodile
Which lures its prey
With deep dimples and bumps

I hope we smile
Like the newly wed
Who shows her dentition
In wait for a TV spot

DOTARD

I hope we don't get stung
By scorpion's sting
Which stiffens our crops
And strangles our rusted hoes

I hope we help, help
Those swept into
The bins of history
Never to be remembered

I hope we smile
I hope we dance
I hope we help
No codes. No cover-ups.

NAMBIA

Don't tell me
You love me
When you can't
Say my name

I am African
Not by blackness
Not by soil
But by birth

I am a queen
Of modernity
From genesis
This has been me

For ages now
Kings praise me
Lords envy me
Yet, you don't know me

DOTARD

You put me
To elastic shame today
At the global congregation
You don't know me

I'm not Nambia
I don't know Nambia
Call me Zambia
Call me Namibia

Those I know
Those I can answer
Queens, they are
And kings lure

Don't tell me
You love me
When you don't know me
My name, you can't say

BLACK CAVAIR

The taste of which
Corrupts the minds
Of men, the smell
Of which blocks
Noses of the *Novaks*
In this culture contest
Though borrowed by
Johnny-come-latelies.
Outlanders. Novitiates. They
Fall into unconscious
Trap of times, set
By spymasters who
Knows the endgame, yet
Go ahead tasting this
Great delicious delicacy, but
Insulated with coated
Taste buds that covers
The marks of the
Black caviar in the
Oily mouth of munchers. They
Intentionally extend this
Relics to gluttonous

Execs who seek to
Stuff further into
Their burgeoning bedchambers
Hoping no crumb falls
Along their footsteps. But
It takes a breath, one
Single inhalation and another
Single exhalation. Trap
Of times. Crime de la crème

DOTARD

Times have changed
Words have too
Yesterday was seminal
Today, asinine
We used to hear
Words filled with wisdom
Now we hear
Scums and destruction
Before, we used to hear
Words with future attached
Now we hear
All things, all ascorbic things
Pronounced without guard
From the pulpit of times
We imagine this
We imagine that
Today is disturbed
With boys and dotards
Today is harmed
By lack of depth
Depth of the past
Past so awash
With tears and fears

Those pasts
Are present
Present with us
Yet, we stare
We let them steer
But we might perish
In this history
Of ours
They might destroy
This time
Of ours
This story
Might be told
By no one
At all
By the time
We wake up
Dawn will be here
Nuclear button pressed
To destroy. To inferno.
What is left of man
Sole purpose
Of a dotard

COVFEFE

As poets, in free verse write
So, presidents, in free form speak
All works of changing climes
All works of changing times
We chime in language different
We tearfully talk down tradition
Making up things from nowhere
Morphing letters and words
Not in meaningful context
Not in convivial content
Verbose not friendly to wordsmith
Rejected in the gospel of Guinness
Abhorred by overmodest onlookers
Yet, we smile and dance
While presidents speak in free
Form, we sit from far away
From tables, we all own.
With hands akimbo and disabled, we
Resign to fate in fear
Waiting for heaven to help us
Praying for divine intervention
In times of old, they matched
In times of old, they smashed

DOTARD

In times of old, they crushed
With spears in hands, they lined
With peers and fears, they rolled
They rose. They spoke. To kings. To lords.
Commoners, they were at that time
Uncommon things they did at their time
Plebiscite, they were at that time
Much power, they brandished at their time
Without wings, they flew and grew
To turn the tides of times
With no tech, they talked and rolled
And travelled to lands unknown
Now we have the wires
The filament that weaved us as
one Yet, we fail to use
Our spears to speak to
peers Yet, we fail to say
The words you speak are frail
It's time to tame the trend
That tries to tear us down

Spiritual

YOUR APPOINTED TIME

The flesh goes before the spirit in an awkward way
Leading things ephemeral instead of things eternal
Caring for temporaries, not things without seasons
Working by sight, not faith
Working with men, not
Him We stumble, we blame
Him We fail, we ask why
We men think so much of Give
us all day our yearly bread
Prayer of the greedy The
usurpers
The egotist
Not prayer of the populist
Be still, and
Know the appointed
Time will come

TAKE IT TO GOD

What if we stop and think
And think of what to take to God
What if we pause and think
And think of how heavy each burden is
What if we stop and think
And think of that it's only one man

He is not a weightlifting man
He is not preparing for a tournament
He is not a juju master
He has no magic fingers
When you take it to Him

The tools to loosen the problems
The keys to unlock your luck
The wisdom to defeat the serpent
The eyes to discern your concerns
The shoulders to carry our worries
He gave us on the sixth day

In His own image and likeness
With His own breath He gave life into us
In His own powers, He gave us power over the devil

He gave us the Holy Spirit to guard us
He gave us His only son for our sins

What if we stop taking it to Him?

What if?

ONLY REMEMBERED

The artifacts
You leave behind
Staunchly stays in place
While its creator
Goes to world
Beyond this place

Your footprints
Stays on lonely
Passageways of life
Only to be
Recalled by histories
Hooks and grippers

The words
You say goes
Miles to touch
Or smooch smiles on million faces
But still damage
Many silent sapiens

The tweets
From your account
Matters a lot
Towards your legacy

Leaving the world
Tattered or taunted

The look
On your faces
When issues of
Importance need attention
But you show
Pretension that will be captured by
Time

Your Instagram posts
Your MySpace posts
Your Facebook posts
Your WhatsApp posts
Your Twitter posts
All show the telling
Stories of you

When you mute
Your vocal cavity
In the sordid face
Of Armageddon
Generation will
Read your empty
Epitaph that says
Nothing about you

DOTARD

Your thoughts
In paper if etched
In proper papyrus
Will last till
The elusive rapture falls upon us

We will
Only be
Remembered by
Our works
On earth
As our days
Begin to dwindle
When we remain dumb to things that count

IS THE WORLD FLAT?

I'm thinking: is the world flat?
Where there are no hills and no hounds?
Where there are no mountains and no mongrels?
Where there are no valleys and no volleys?
Is the world really flat as I'm thinking?

If the world is flat, there would be symmetry
of speech and no spook
If the world is flat, there would be tandem
of thoughts and no trough
If the world is flat, there would be angels all
around and no antagonist
If the world is really flat

I think, if the world is flat, there will be no waters
to cross and no waves to fight
I think, if the world is flat, there will be no sky to fly
in and no hiccups to experience
I think, if the world is flat, there will be no bombs
to blast and no nuclear weapons to test I'm
thinking: this world isn't flat

LOVENUTS

Of that seed, that forbidden seed, that turned
man into a zombie of sorts
Of that inamorata, that inamorata, that twisted
the head of our first Adam and sucked it dry
Dry till today; dry now; dry till eternity; until the
second coming of the resurrection and life;
when that will be
Not only that we became dry, we have been left
with punishment of death; to give up the soul and
spirit; to never return to earth same; except to
reincarnate; if that will be
A condemnation brought down on us by
disobedience; not putting our ears to the
ground; not hearing the silent voice that comes
once in a leap year; if you will hear
It is that thirst; that greed; that pushed us out of
Eden and brought us into Sodom and we still
swallow the fruit in and out and still walk in
darkness every day of our lives
We quashed that first favor; the favor of the
creator; the maker of heaven; the maker of earth

We traded that humanity; heavenly humanity;
free gift from high for simple seductive spree
Like the great *Iroko* tree cut down by multiple blades
of a hews man, we dropped; from grace to grass and
have remained on the grass and still mowed with
newer lawn-mower; a happy upgrade for man
Battling with devil and evil in every step of the way
Quarreling with brothers and sisters for every little
fray
Giving our lives for nothing by the seconds by
the day
Only because we dropped from grace into a
winter-looking grass
Signifying rejection from on high; thrown down
from the upmost throne
Rejection of creation by many apostates who
think this creation is a façade; the
Illogicality risen from a certain Eve speaking to
a certain serpent; dialogue of sorts
And the rejectionists ask: what snake speaks?
What human hears? Isn"t that illogical?
As crafty as the serpent; as dumb as a human
And the human was beguiled; deceived into
plucking the apple and further;

And the woman was beguiled; deceived into
giving the apple to the man; and further
All sounds metaphorical; conjured up; doesn"t
add up; story of control
Of the mind; good for morals; unfit for now
For now is evil everywhere; condemnation thrown
at people
As if we"ve got the condemnation rights as a people
Saying you are right; he is wrong
Wrong for making a life choice
Making them have no proven voice
But now with some support they rejoice
The right to choose becoming a non-
fundamental human right
All circles back to disobedience; fallen from grace
to grass; and staying there till the end of time
Signaling end of time; the floods; the fornications;
the fiendishness; the flagitiousness but no fire
Existence of war; nations over nations; fiefdom
kicking kingdoms but not really
All because of disobedience; all because of
lacking discernment; all because of the love nuts.

HOW THINGS ARE

You are the dream I dream
That comes into existence at dawn
When all is said, and all is done

You are the tall tree
In the deep mangrove that I tap
Which brings forth saccharine tasting whitish
liquid At cockcrow that satisfies my soul

You are the moon that dims the darkness in me
And ushers in brightness in the morning
With your rising east shine

You are the silence that sneaks into my
ears When the city has gone to sleep
And the early hours buzzing that wakes me up
When the trucks drive through the highways

You are the one who shield my heart as troubles
trail my butt
And the unseen spirit that shapes my soul when
the bustling starts

DOTARD

You are my early-morning flower
That unfurls with saintly jasmine-like fragrance in the
evening
And shuts down as soon as the early
sunrise"s trumpet sounds

You are the little buzz
I set before I close my eyes
Which in turn wakes me up when I did not set
it again in the sunup

That's
Just
How
It
Is

You are the pull that
Pulls me back to the recliner when I'm done and
out of strength
And the push that
Pushes me out of bed
To go and struggle for the daily bread

DOTARD

You are the yin
That adds that dark color to my day
And reinforces me the next with a yang
Which propels my future into Eldorado

You are that duality
That deftly defines why I'm on earth
And reminds me that there are skills I have
that could be used to save a life
Just, save a life, one day at a time

That's
Just
How
It
Is

DEEP IN LOVE

To lean on you
Is what I pray
To hold and touch
Tip of your robe
To sing and say
It's you I love
To tell them all
You loved me first
To you I am
To you I come
My knees I bow
To you my love
Take me, take all
I give you all
The song in me
Is all of praise
O, Lord, my love
My love is deep

CHROMATIN

If asked
To choose,
To choose
Some one:
It's you
It'll be.
If forced
To call,
To call
A name:
It"s you,
Your name:
Your name
I'll call.

You are
The core.
You are
The rock.
You are
The bread.
The life
Of me.

The head.
The tail.
You are
In me.
For me,
You came.

The hedge
For me.
The tree
Of me.
The quench
For taste.
The rock
Of all.
Your branch,
I am. You
gave To
me, The
ribs From
you.

Age to age,
You are
The same.

Sea to sea,
Your name
Is praised.
Time to time,
Your name
Is same.
Coast to coast,
The rock
You are.
My cornerstone,
End to end.

If asked
To choose,
Your name
I'll choose.
When forced
To name,
Your name
I'll scream.
With joy
In me,
Your name

I'll praise.
End to end,
Still it's you.

MY TIME

Bitter shame and sorrow
Baggage of night and day
All it brings today
And tomorrow, yet to come

Day by day, alone
Pains from folks we know
Callous in thoughts and deeds
Saints they clone all day

Deeper they dig and dodge
Higher they soil and sing
Eternity for me I earn
And leave us all to yawn

THE TESTAMENT
(Inspired by Bidwell Okere)

In a few words
Your works, your
Deeds will be

Only sweet words,
Will they say, your
Life was in a way

By then, deep
Huge sleep would have
Wrapped you with sand

Passers-by will, by
Then know, there
Was a man

Tell me now, those
Sweet words that will
Live with me till eternity

Social

CRACKHEADS

Take a walk around the block
See some sinners in their act
Do some things you cannot do
The sane detest and rightly so
At the glare of all they post their shame
In the dark alley, they skim and sport
Same today, same always
All the same, despite all help
Same old sport in same old spot

GIRLY GENERATION

This age is precarious
Seating on a precipice
Driving off the tangent
On a second-by-second basis

This youth is dangerous
Tutored by misguided men
Trading their unfortunate wares
Against the wishes of us all

My generation is doomed
Doomed by our unmanliness
And castrated to nothingness
And we remain messed up for real

We recline on docility
And remain so even in the eyes of many storms
We are wimps and cry always
And not put up a battle for us

I LOVE YOU

When I met you, I was still young, still tender,
still striking, still blameless
What I love most in you was you, your soul,
your innocence, your calm
Your soul was cool, very cool and calm, very calm
You were loved by many, street sleepers and
plum gatherers
You gave them what they sought in you, in
your shrine, in your abode
They became repeat offenders, coming over,
and over again
You got them hooked by the juice which comes
from your raps and wraps
They breathed the harsh sweet aroma which
comes from all angles
Your air was hot, damn hot but still provided
me much calm
Your soul rooted in soulful tunes of yesteryears,
yes now, and years to come
Your gentle rascality was misread by fools and
fools they remain

You"ve shown me the best in you, and I
understood your beats you send
I knew your rhythm, your tempo and captured all
the stanzas of you
The chorus consumes not only me, but dwellers
and wailers into the world of ours
Our zone, my zone was ours, no mine letting no
one distract my affection to you
You drew me into your heart with your beats and
flutes, drums and gongs, saxophones and trumpets
They permeated into my soul and cloned my soul
to yours
I was open to you even when I was young, I am
still open to you now that I am old
Even when they castrated you, you still filled me,
you still satisfied me
With what was left of you before they took you
away from me
Your handsomeness, your fitted frame,
your vociferous voice
Your baritone beams into my membrane
and provides my aching soul with serenity
I become so jealous when others say your name
and say, "I love you" and scream and shout
But I know you love me and only me you love

DOTARD

You talk to me and take me down the lanes of
old And bring me into present
And still projects me into the future
You whisper into my ears the truth in you that
makes them hate you so much
You caress my body and dress it with the reality
that stares us in the eyes today
You foretold these realities but we never took
you serious
They called you rascal, vagabond, no-good-
child, over-fed by parents" wealth
You told the true story
Just myself, the one you love, and your followers
who you love too but love me most Understood you,

You didn"t talk to me about money, you didn"t talk
to me about wealth
You didn"t talk to me about butts, you didn"t talk
to me about titties
That made me respect you so much, that made
me let you seat on my heart
You walked me through the walls of my
campuses, home and abroad
In my ears came your lyrics as I was about to snap
a picture with John Harvard

And the telegraphic tales of your gong walked me back to the Great *Ikenga* halls in *Uturu* Reminding me of the cashews, the across the gate *kpunkpus*, the ring-road
You spoke to me about our struggles
You spoke to me about their orgies
We struggle because they have strangled all the strength in us and we become castrated
They ravish and revel in our stupidity and incapacitation and inabilities and handicaps They still do...
I am talking about you Afrobeat King. King Fela Anikulapo Kuti

PEACE, PERFECT, PEACE

Clash, perfect clash,
In this space, we call ours
The blood of children curse all that have brought
us shame

Clash, perfect, clash
In every clime and time
The worlds are seeing all senseless dualities

Clash, perfect, clash
In times, this, troubled times
The storms are raging every mile and clime

Clash, perfect, clash
Is what we hear all times
Of those that think they have this world as theirs

Clash, perfect, clash
Our future still unknown
Our fates are grounded by these shameless men

DOTARD

Clash, perfect, clash
With sorrow all o'er us
Our hands, lands varnish in as we go to sleep

Clash, perfect, clash
With these dark deriders
They have now filled our consciousness with full filth

Clash, perfect, clash
No end in sight right now
Until we stand, shout and scream them out

I'M REVVED UP

I'm revved up
Revved up to
Spit out stuff
At the faces
Of my traitors

I'm revved up
To say to
My deadened detractors
My shit cannot
Be messed with

I know I'm
Fully revved up
Like the apostles
At the final
Feast of tabernacle

You know when
You receive your
Spirit to spit
Out shitty stuff

Your tongue twisters
Your mouth mumbles

It's called the
Baptism of beatitude
When the spirit
In you is
Bigger than the
Gin in them

It's called the
Anointing of the
Shitty spirit, when
You recognize that
Larger voice tucked
Inside of your
Guttural pipeline and
Let it go

Let it go
The shitty spirit
Let it flow
The reverend voice

Let it rev
Nothing like it
Let it go

I'M LIKE

I'm like
This character isn't ours
It seems like a Greek gift
And should be returned as such

I'm like,
This madness doesn't run in us
So, the witches who cooked this
Should be made to nullify it

I'm like,
When has it been that we have lost the giant status
We should do everything to regain our prestige

I'm like,
When has our grammar degenerated to this
disdain A total turn away from our trademark
Queens English

A NEW LEAF

I've turned
A new Leaf,
like The
autumn Leaf
turns After it's
Turn of The
season: The
season The
forerunner To
summer
Summer so So
green

You gave
Me a
New heart
When the
Doctors have
Declared me
Vegetative: no
Blood running
In my

Veins, but
You came
You came
And gave
Me, gave
Me a
Fab life
 A life
So free

The breath
In me
Smells like
A newly Minted
cologne Fresh
on
The shelves
At the Prime
of Ecstasy:
when All
shine
All glow So
glorious So
green

I'm now
Trimmed to
Tuxedo-like
Suit: the
Tailor in
Your measured
Hands produced
These new
Clothes, making
Me a
New wine
In a
New wine
Skin: so
So fresh

I can't Wait
to Go into
The world
Stand on The
rooftops
Shout and
Proclaim
your
Goodness in

My life:
Putting in
Me, a
New man
And taking
The old
Adam away
So far
Away from
Me.

IT'S ALL ABOUT ANGLES
(Inspired by Attorney Chris Aguocha)

Life districts
Separate east
From west
North from
South and
Set each
Entity apart
Making each
Azimuth tough
To reach

Each life
Stump stops
At angles
Dreamed and
Angles undreamed
Tossing toppling
All trajectories
Seeking some
Ways out

DOTARD

At the
Corners of
Life's junction
You talk
Your way
In or
Your way
Out, seeking
Suiting angles
To hang
In on
At each
Given phase

It's all
About angles
Some tough
Some rough
Others smooth
Others smart
It takes
Kismet to
Get on

DOTARD

The right
Life angle
It's really
All about
Life angles

SLEEP

Sleep
Sleep, my little doll
It is a call
You have to heed

Sleep
Sleep, don't fight
It all
You can't deny a kid his toy

Sleep
Sleep, to wake
In time
You have to do
Sleep time again
Sleep my little darling

I AM THE STORM
(Inspired by Hon. Maria Ude Nwachi)

I am the storm
I am the storm that wrenches a man's treasure and
crushes it into shreds and scraps and signs my
ugly signature on the sand dunes for visitors to
know I was here
I am the storm
I am the storm that comes unpublished even when
meteorologists have planned to track me down
with their false-tools and deceiving people with
wrong predictions and make them crash in the still
snow of Colorado
I am the storm
The storm that cuts across landmarks, east west
north south cities up countries hinterlands upper
lands sanctuaries synagogues on Sabbaths on
Sundays pursuing kneelers who prostrate to
god's unknown and unseen: unanswered prayers
I am the storm
That tells the devil that I am the storm when he tries
to make me bow before him for me to inherit the
earth and not make heaven when the time comes

and works forty days and forty nights without
food to break me when he knows I am the storm I
am the storm
That rages in perpetuum, winter summer fall autumn
harmattan rainy season and fear no fall because I've
been rooted like the northern star and mount Zion
that cannot be moved from its location till the end of
time
I am the storm
The storm that beheads the beauty of your
handsomeness scythes your tall decency dotting
down streets and boulevards, impersonating
chimerical colors across this shore and luring
the innocents into incremental servitude I am
the storm
That storm that surges seriously over the oceans
and carries ocean debris and river flunks and flips
them on top your razor-lined clean-shaved
shimmering-looking hair and rips down your power
line of ego I am the storm
The storm that squeezes out tears from your rigid
eyes and with my squad guards no internal or
external hands to come cleanse your whimpering
for we mount sentry at every point of contact

I am the storm, the storm that defiles
definite predictions
I am the storm, the storm that defines new rules
of engagement
I am the storm, the storm that
depresses longstanding traditions of old
I am the storm, the storm that says that I am
the storm I am the storm.

ELOI, ELOI

I screamed
My Love
My Love
Why have
You forsaken me

But He
Did not
Abandon me
Nor forsake me
But he
Did, he
And not He

His hush
Ego pushes
Him around
Like the
Little wind
That tosses
Lightweight paper
Up in the air
To prove

DOTARD

He's the
Head of
The house
He orders
Me in
And out
Like the
Soldier commanding
His battalion
In readiness
For parade

I thought He
was My lord I
thought He was
My love But he
Was that
Proverbial
green Snake
hidden In the

Green grass
His trueness

Was torpedoed
By my
Eagerness to
Be me
Chased out
Of his
Hole by
The redness
In me
Like the
Furnace to
A snake

My love
He was not
My lord
He was not
My true love
Never left
Me dry
My real Lord
Never let
Me down

My Lord
Eloi
You never
Lama sabachthani
But he
Did to
Me what
The Jews
Did to
My Lord

NEAR NAKED

I had a thought
Of seeing you naked
And people preying on you

I had an imagination
Where you were supine
They stole from you

I saw your painting
On public gallery
They poked and choked

They prey on
Your reckless practice
Of abandonment

They stole from
Your solid hands
Of oil and gas

They poked on
Your bare face
Of insecurity and solitude

DOTARD

I saw you
Near naked at
The global beach

All but you
Clothed
All but you
Covered
All but you
Careful

I saw you flaunt
Your stupidity in
Public air and glare

BLANK

I have come to accept
The understanding that man
Is so sadly destined
To the starless midnight
Of racism and war that
The bright daybreak of peace and
Brotherhood can never
Become a reality, and
I believe that unarmed truth and
Unconditional love will
Have the final word

REFLECTION

There"s a time in life
When we feel comfortable with our way of life
Stop. Look in the rearview mirror
And see what she tells you

Your reflection gives a lot of information
And her judgment, so sound so clear
If you can break out from your shellshock
You will certainly hear what she should tell

She tells you that she"s your alter ego
Your final arbiter. A chip off the old block
And the one who will determine your future.
She is the fellow who tells you as it is

She"s the heart that never leaves your body
Always attached to you like a set of twins
She"s the rib of your rib, the bone of your bone
The prophecy of the old

Page | 147

DOTARD

You may, in all your life, make a jest of many
And, in many times, flee unscathed with it
But the scars will fill your brain
As soon as you lie to yourself

LOCKED UP

I"m mired in this deep dump,
This slum of slime and blame.
It's known to breed odd things:
Peasants, plebeians and peons.

Way deep inside this dump,
Lay gold, dough and brooch.
Dug by just a few monsters,
With tools offbeat and loony.

Most, made to choke us all, and
Keep the mine for them.
I"m stumped in this core dump,
With balls, shushed and gagged.

I've got to dust my lines, and
Make them clear and straight.
This dump, we can drain, If
you can hum my lines.

PALM 23

Like grown sheep, we all are fed,
Yet, we lack in everything
On soft beds, we always lay
But our backs, just hurt as hell
Every sec, we walk astray
Still we pray in His only name
We prostrate each passing day
To god's unknown in dark valley
When evil come our many ways
Comfort runs, like big old dear
Our table always look unkempt
With many maids that never sleep
Our foes spit and despise us
In the presence of the most high
Oil on our feet, are washed away,
Washed away by shaky faith
Roughness, sadness follow us
Every way we set our steps
And we dwell in the house of hell
Until death do us part.

ALL THINGS BRIGHT AND BEAUTIFUL

All things are bright, ha-ha,
All things are beautiful, yes
Because you are not
Born where I was born
Because you don't feel
What I've always felt
Because you've never
Seen what I've seen, just
Writing in prose, from
Your closet of comfort
Penning down imagery, and
Folklore conjured up in
Your crack-filled head, you
Think that washers, and
Dryers, you think that microwave
And heaters can be equated
To basins and ropes, and
You think that Xcel energy
is What it is called where I
Come from, no, we have the
Powerful never expect power always, now
renamed, power house con nation, you think that
Internet is the same as using

Gong at the dusk of time to
Transmit to 150 million
Starved souls, that the president
Will be in town and everyone
Should bring yams, and
10 cups of groundnut, all
Things being bright, being
Beautiful. No, you got it all
Wrong, all things, everything, even
Things that were supposed to be
Bright, and those things that
Were supposed to be beautiful, they
Were all, all things dark and ugly, the
Face, the smile, the handshake, all
Were dark and ugly, all con,
All held back by barons of the
land, All dark, all ugly
You constantly castrate her efforts
To becoming beautiful, you've
Colluded with the continuous changing faces,
and robbed her of
Her innocence, her sense vacuumed by
unnecessary vaccination

To rid her of her beauty, and now you recline in your
Wheelchair, receiving your pension
For old age is a good thing

HEARTBREAKING

(For my good friend, Wellington Ogude, who lost his loving wife, Dioma)

Dusk is set on dear one
And you are left to mourn her
This has been a tough one
But it has made you dearer
At times like this you lose it
But think of what she told you
Make her feel you know her
And do the things she told you
Her kids, your kids are all there
You have to make them know that
She told you things about them
To love, to hold at all times
Keep your head in safe place
And make it sane as ever
It is the time you have to
Care, and do the right things
For her, for you, and your kids
It's hard to do but you should,
Do the things she told you
Be there for her as you've been

And she will smile to heaven
The two of you were lovebirds
And she will love you always
She came and saw and conquered
And you should do the other things
Your friends are here to cheer you
And say they will forever
Your faith is what will hold you
And trust in Him at all times
She's gone to rest for long time
And we'll all meet one day
Wish her well on her trip
As she will be your angel
She knows you love her so much
And you will always do
She knows you'll care for her kids
And she will fear of nothing
Put your trust in Lord God, and
Wish her well on this trip

I HAVE A DREAM

I have a dream
That one day
My sweet daughter
Will go back
To her fatherland
And an anopheles
Mosquito will bite her
And she will ask me,
What was that, on my skin?
I have a dream.
I have a dream,
That very soon,
My only child
Will visit where
Her parents come from,
And there will be
No running water,
And power holding
Will seize light for
months, And one day,
She will learn to scream
"There is light,"
And light will dim

At the apex of her excitement.
I have a dream.
I have a dream,
That in less than no time,
I will take my sweetness
To an air conditioned airport,
And she will fly so smoothly,
But when the air smells
Her fatherland, heat from
Nowhere, will welcome her,
Then she will know
There is something called
An African ingenuity
Where things are made out of nothing.
I have a dream.
I have a dream,
That one day,
My very angel
Will stop a taxi
On *Balogun* street
And the cabman's
Waze traffic app
Will not work,
And she finds herself,
In Ouagadougou.

Which is no where
Near her fatherland,
But that's her lesson
In African geography.
I have a dream.
I have a dream,
That one day,
My daughter will
Want to go
To her maternal home,
And on her way,
She will be stopped by
Thousands of police checks,
And she will be asked,
To part with some money
For using phonetics
On ill-uniformed policemen,
And she will be bewildered,
And speak more phonetics,
And they will welcome her,
By asking my American child
To write a statement,
At the police station

With her own pen,
And her own paper.
I have a dream.

FATHER McMAHON

It has come
It has passed
It's the story
Of one reverend
A reverend father
Father so pious
So we thought
Naive we were
It may have been
Naive we were
Not until now
For now we know
What they all do
Let's not go there
For you all know
But all in all
It's still a story
Of one reverend
A reverend father, and
Time has come, and
Time has passed
When then as kids
Ball race was fun

But in those days
We find solace
Our manmade kites
We dreamt of the future
When we all will
To the future fly
Skies of fortune
Skies so blue, but
Here we are
In McMahon's land
Maybe it was
His hands we shook
Maybe it was
Our hands unwashed
Maybe it was
Our childish chastity
Maybe it was
Our manmade kites
For we believed
When we touched this,
McMahon's hands, and
Not wash them,
To heaven we'll go
For we all thought
We had touched "god"

And here's our heaven
In a land we thought
Was made of gold
In a land so blessed
But still cursed
We slapped his hands
McMahon's hands
While he drove pass
His white Peugeot
So very white
Like priestly robe
Which we thought
Was a great healer
For we thought
A touch of his hands
Will save us all
For we hoped
A touch of his robe
Will set us free
I still remember
A man so pure
A man so nice
Father McMahon

A BROKE WORLD

We now live
In a world so broke
Lust and love
Lost in the lanes

Things that made
Us what we were
Tossed and thrown
Deep down the drain

Man is now
His own kill sport
Turns against
His own goodwill

The things we seek
Makes us so sick
The things we chase
Are all vain things

DOTARD

Here we are
Nowhere to turn
Here we are
No one to save

Pain and pang
Peel our thick skins
Sore and stain
Fill our big hearts

Blood and blame
Is now our game
We seat and watch
All gains get zapped

Let's unite
And pull our purse
Fill its vault
With peace and love

POET TO POET

Effervescent transcendence
Of diction and dreams.
Luring appurtenances
Of lyrics and romance.
Interlocking thoughts,
Traversing traditions
And trends and times.
Mystical congregation
Of kindred spirits
In places so hidden, and
Spots so sophisticated.
Trafficking mumbo jumbo,
Things that make no
Literal sense to streets men
And statesmen
Invocation of tattered hearts.
Supplication for jiggered souls.
Tossing lifeless limbs
Across ladders and bridges.
Adding oxygen into blocked
Nostrils and bones begin
To rise again. Yes, bones
Begin to rise in places

So tortured with thistles
And lands touched with
Sledgehammer and knuckled manure.

SCULPTURING

Like snake
Which hisses
Which flickers
Its tongue
Like snake
With its
Legless elongation
And flexible
Scaly skin
Like snake
Which eats
Rodents, eats
Termites, and
Eats reptiles
Like snake
Which hides
In between
Dark crevices
And huge
Tree branches
Pointing to
Diverse directions
Like snake

The ectotherms
You tan
And retreat
You genuflect
And hibernate
Yet, continue
To survive
The torture
That comes
With in
And out
Bodily movements
You enjoy
The conviviality
And, sometimes
The roughness
That comes
With the
Rugged terrains
Yet, you
Go back
The next
Day, to

Fight another
Day to
Cherish the
Sweetness of it

ECC 7290

Here comes the moonlight,
We circled there.
Ready for the stories
Told by royal elders.
Of tortoise and his shell.
The moon and the axe man.
No Xbox, no Twitter
Our voice was the tweet.
We talked, we did not text
We ate, from one same pot.
Tales by the moonlight
A name with a reason.
You never miss a session
The cane will be waiting.
No whistling in the night,
Or spirits will come get you.
No looking to your left side,
Or the dead will all wake up.
Burial ground was sacred,
Not cemetery of these days.
When someone was real dead
We knew he'll come as spirit
These days we drink and merry

DOTARD

When someone lies in state.
It's all a moonlight tale,
Told by reverend elders.
Our children will not know this,
Unless we told them so.
But, we all are way too busy
Chasing name, fame and wealth.
What story will they tell,
Tales by the Twitter.
What tale will they share,
News from their Xbox.
Give me back my glory,
Drive me back to yore.
ECC is waiting
The 7, and 2, and ninety.
Take me back to those days,
I want my moonlight tales.

SOLITUDE

The frequent
Travel of
The deranged.
The journey
Of the
Distorted,
Who stands
Solitary in
The middle
Of an
Ocean, and
Sees everyone
Swimming at
The bed
Of this
Mangled sea.
A hero
He becomes.
Pulling variegated
Sinking hands
As turbulence
And tide
Walk across

The undulating
Surface of
This raging
Waters. Yet,
This journeyman
Stands still,
Waving at
Images, shouting
Uncountable incantations
At his
Innermost spirit
That none
Sees, except
Himself.
World of
One. Where
Kids and
Kindred men,
Peers and
Parents exist
Not. World
Where everything
Tumbles, crumbles
On this
Illusion-draped king

And no
Tribesman runs
To rescue.
And he
Reclines to
His reclusive
Emblem.

Made in the USA
Monee, IL
26 October 2022

16593067R00104